Around the Neighborhood

HOUGHTON MIFFLIN HARCOURT
School Publishers

Contents

Dan and Nan

by Evan MacDonald
illustrated by Lorinda Bryan Cauley

I am Dan Cat.

Dan Cat sat.

I am Nan Cat.

Nan Cat sat.

Dan sat. Nan sat.

Dan and Nan can play.

Nat Cat

by Uta Tibi
illustrated by Noah Jones

Nat Cat sat.

Nan sat.

Tad sat.

Nan can play with Tad.

Nat! Nat! Nat Cat!

Nan, Tad, and Nat can play.

Nan and Dan

by Donald Busch
illustrated by Rick Powell

Nan can tap a pan.

Nan can help Dan tap.

Dan can tap and tap!

Nan can pat a cat.

Dan can pat the cat.

The fat cat can nap.

Dan can nap with Nan.

Fan, Fan, Fan
by Graham Neu

Pat sat. Pat can be a fan.
Fan, fan, fan, fan.

Dan sat. Dan can be a fan.
Fan, fan, fan, fan.

Nan sat. Nan can be a fan.
Fan, fan, fan, fan.

Sam sat. Sam can be a fan.
Fan, fan! Fan, fan!

Pam sat.   Pam can be a fan.
Fan, fan!   Fan, fan!

Can you be a fan?
Fan! Fan! Fan! Fan!

Can It Fit?

by Chandra Majors

illustrated by Elizabeth Allen

It is a tan cap.

What can fit in it?

A fan can fit in it.
Is it for a fan?

A tin pan is in it.
Is it for a tin pan?

A map can fit in it.
Is it for a map?

Ram Cat can sit in it.
Is it for Ram Cat?

Look at Sam!
It is his cap.
Ram is his cat.

I Ran

by Chris Gericho

Pam ran.
Tif did, too.

Dad is with Pat.

Dad ran. Pat ran.

Sid ran, ran, ran.
Tip is with him.

Look at Tim.

Tim ran. Nan did, too.

Dan ran, ran, ran!
Tam ran. Cam did, too.

I ran, ran, ran!
Did you?

Sid Pig

by Damian Byrne
illustrated by Ethan Long

Look at Sid Pig.
He can see a big fig.

It is a fat fig, too!

Can Sid tap the big, fat fig?

Can Sid tip the big, fat fig?

Can Sid hit the big, fat fig?

Sid Pig did it!
Sid can have his fig.

Sid bit his big, fat fig.
Mmm! Mmm!

Pam

by Tony Manero
illustrated by Jeff Shelly

Tip has a bat.
It is for Pam.

Did Pam bat?
Pam sat!

Rip has a cap.

It is for Pam.

Pam has a cap!
Pam has a bat, too.

Pam is at bat.
Can Pam hit it?

Bam! Pam did it!
It is a big, big hit!

Lil and Max

by Alexis Davis
illustrated by Akemi Gutierrez

Lil got a big, big mop.
Can Lil and Max sit on top?

Can they do it? No!

Max got a big, big pot.
Can Lil and Max hop on it?

Hip, hop. Hip, hop, hop.
Lil and Max hop in it!

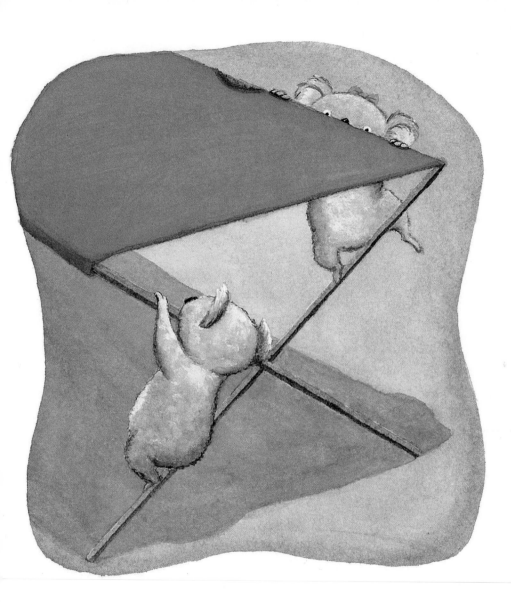

Lil and Max find a cot.
It is a big, big, BIG cot!

Lil can sit on top!

Max can sit on top, too!

Did Dix Dog Do It?

by Oliver Berry
illustrated by Mike Gordon

Dad Dog is sad.
Dad has to fix it.
Did Dix Dog do it?

Sal Dog is sad.
Did Dix Dog do it?

Mom Dog is sad.

It is not funny!

Did Dix Dog do it?

Lon Dog is sad.
Did Dix Dog do it?

Doc Dog is sad.
Did Dix Dog do it?

No! Max Cat did it!

Max Fox and Lon Ox

by David McCoy
illustrated by Kristin Sorra

Max Fox is six.

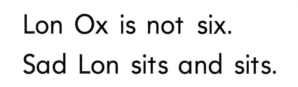

Lon Ox is not six.
Sad Lon sits and sits.

Max got a big box.
It is a big, big box!
What is in it?

It is a sax!

Max plays. Bip, bop!

Bip, bop, bop, bop!

Can Lon Ox play?   No!
What can Lon Ox do?

Lon Ox can sing!

Is It Funny?

by Laurence Christopher

illustrated by Liz Callen

Pat can tap.

Pat taps, taps, taps.

Hal is not sad.
Hal sits in his box.

Ron Dog is hot.
Pat fans the hot dog.

Hal can sing.
Hal sings a rap.

Pat has a big pot.
Pat can mix a lot.

Hal has a pad.

What is on it?

It is funny!

Pals

by Aiden Brandt

Len and his pals can hop!
Len led all his pals.

Lin has a pet dog.
Wags is a pal!

Wes let his pals in.

His pals can play in his den.

Can Mom be a pal?
Yes! Mom and Ben get logs.

Six pals ran six laps.
Who led the pals? Mel did!

Ted sat on a big log.
Ted sat with his pals.

Ned

by David McCoy
illustrated by Neena Chawla

Here is Ned.
Who is he?

Ned is not Ned Pig.
Ned is not Ned Ox.
Ned is Ned Hog.

Is Ned Hog big? Yes!
Does Ned have ten wigs? No!
Ned Hog has ten hats!

Ned has a cap, too.
Ned Hog is at bat.
Can he get a big hit? Yes!

Ned Hog is hot.

It is not hot in here.

Ned can nap in his bed.

Who is Ned Hog?
Ned is top hog!
Ned wins, wins, wins!

Ken and Vic

by Kate Pistone
illustrated by Deborah Melmon

Here is Ken.
Here is Vic.

Ken gets his bat.
What does Vic get?

Can Ken get a hit?
Yes! It is a big hit!
Top job, Ken!

Can Vic get it?
Yes! Vic tags Ken!
Top job, Vic!

Ken gets his tan bag.
Vic gets his bag with dots.

Ken has a big wet sip.
Vic has a sip, too.
Top job, Ken and Vic!

My Pets

by Alice Ling
illustrated by Meryl Treatner

Big Vic is my pet dog.
Kit is my pet cat.

Kit can get six red jets.
Get the jets, Kit!

Big Vic can get ten tin men.
Here, Big Vic. Get set. Go!

Kit and Big Vic nap in the den.
Kit and Big Vic nap with me.

Big Vic and Kit get fed.
Sit, Big Vic, sit!

Kit fits in the cat bed.
Big Vic does not fit in it.
Big Vic does not fit in my bed!

Fun in the Sun

by Norman Swaderski
illustrated by Stephen Lewis

Jen Pig is hot.
Can Jen hop in? No!

Ed Hog is hot.
Can Ed hop in? Yes!
Ed has fun, fun, fun!

Ed pulls his friend.
Tug, tug. Hold on, Jen.

Can Jen hop in? Yes!
Jen has fun, fun, fun!

Ed Hog hops up, up, up!
Jen Pig hops up, up, up!

Ed has fun in the sun.
Jen has fun in the sun, too!

Yams! Yum!

by Rona Blanca
illustrated by Gina Freschet

Yak is in bed,
but he has to get up.

Yak has to get yams.
What can Yak do?

Can Yak get big, fat yams?
Yes! He can get lots and lots.

Yak can set his yams in a bag.
His red bag can hold lots!

Yak can fit ten yams in his bag.
His bag is full. Yams! Yum!

Yak has his yams.
He has lots and lots.
Yams! Yum, yum, yum!

Fun, Fun, Fun!

by Harriet Smith

Kim can hold on to Mom.
It is fun, fun, fun!

Bud and Jim zig and zag.
It is fun, fun, fun!

Liz and Jen run.

It is fun, fun, fun!

Deb and Gus play tag.
It is fun, fun, fun!

Ted can play with Dad.
It is fun, fun, fun!

Do not quit! Have fun!
Have fun, fun, fun!

Bud

by David McCoy
illustrated by Jeffrey Ebbeler

Bud is a pug. Bud is a pup.
Bud can fit in a big cup!

Bud digs in the mud.
Quit it, Bud! Quit it!

Zip! Bud hops in the tub.

Rub, rub! Rub-a-dub-dub!

Bud has fun!

Bud sits with us.
We play. Bud naps.

Bud can help us.
Bud gets many hugs!

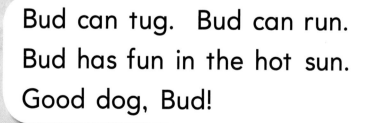

Bud can tug. Bud can run.
Bud has fun in the hot sun.
Good dog, Bud!

Word Lists

Accompanies
"What Is a Pal?"

Dan and Nan

page 3

Decodable Words
Target Skill: Short *a*
am, can, Cat, Dan, Nan, sat

Target Skills: Consonants *n, d*
can, Dan, Nan

High-Frequency Words
New
and, play

Previously Taught
I

Nat Cat

page 9

Decodable Words
Target Skill: Short *a*
can, Cat, Nan, Nat, sat, Tad

Target Skills: Consonants *n, d*
can, Nan, Nat, Tad

High-Frequency Words
New
and, play, with

LESSON 1

Nan and Dan

page 15

Decodable Words
Target Skill: Short *a*
can, cat, Dan, fat, Nan, nap, pan, pat, tap

Target Skills: Consonants *p, f*
fat, nap, pan, pat, tap

Target Skills: Consonants *n, d*
can, Dan, Nan, nap, pan

High-Frequency Words
New
and, help with

Previously Taught
a, the

Fan, Fan, Fan

page 21

Decodable Words
Target Skill: Short *a*
can, Dan, fan, Nan, Pam, Pat, Sam, sat

Target Skills: Consonants *p, f*
fan, Pam, Pat

Target Skills: Consonants *n, d*
fan, can, Dan, Nan

High-Frequency Words
New
be, you

Previously Taught
a

Can It Fit?   page 27

Decodable Words
Target Skill: Short *i:*
fit, his, in, is, it, sit, tin

Target Skills: Consonants *r, h, /z/s*
his, is, Ram

Words with Previously Taught Skills
at, can, cap, Cat, fan, map, pan, Sam, tan

High-Frequency Words
New
for, look, what

Previously Taught
a

I Ran   page 33

Decodable Words
Target Skill: Short *i*
did, him, is, Sid, Tif, Tim, Tip

Target Skills: Consonants *r, h, /z/s*
him, is, ran

Words with Previously Taught Skills
at, Cam, Dad, Dan, Nan, Pam, Pat, Tam

High-Frequency Words
New
look, too

Previously Taught
I, with, you

Sid Pig

Decodable Words

Target Skill: Short *i*
big, bit, did, fig, his, hit, is, it, Pig, Sid, tip

Target Skills: Consonants *b, g*
big, bit, fig, Pig

Target Skills: Consonants *h, /z/s*
his, is

Words with Previously Taught Skills
at, can, fat, Mmm, tap

High-Frequency Words

New
he, have, look, too

Previously Taught
a, see, the

Pam

Decodable Words

Target Skill: Short *i*
big, did, hit, is, it, Rip, Tip

Target Skills: Consonants *b, g*
bam, bat, big

Target Skills: *r, h, /z/s*
has, hit, is, Rip

Words with Previously Taught Skills
at, can, cap, Pam, sat

High-Frequency Words

New
for, too

Previously Taught
a

Lil and Max
page 51

Decodable Words
Target Skill: Short *o*
cot, got, hop, mop, on, pot, top

Target Skills: Consonants *l, x*
Lil, Max

Words with Previously Taught Skills
big, can, hip, in, is, it, sit

High-Frequency Words
New
do, find, no, they

Previously Taught
a, and, too

Did Dix Dog Do It?
page 57

Decodable Words
Target Skill: Short *o*
Doc, Dog, Lon, Mom, not

Target Skills: Consonants *l, x*
Dix, fix, Lon, Max, Sal

Words with Previously Taught Skills
Cat, Dad, did, has, is, it, sad

High-Frequency Words
New
do, funny, no

Previously Taught
to

Max Fox and Lon Ox
page 63

Decodable Words
Target Skill: Short *o*
bop, box, Fox, got, Lon, not, Ox

Target Skill: Inflection *-s*
sits, plays

Target Skills: Consonants *l, x*
box, Fox, Lon, Max, Ox, sax, six

Words with Previously Taught Skills
big, bip, can, in, is, it, sad

High-Frequency Words
New
do, no, sing

Previously Taught
a, and, play, plays, what

Is It Funny?
page 69

Decodable Words
Target Skill: Short *o*
box, Dog, dog, hot, lot, not, on, pot, Ron

Target Skill: Inflection *-s*
fans, sings, sits, taps

Target Skills: *l, x*
box, Hal, lot, mix

Words with Previously Taught Skills
big, can, has, his, in, is, it, pad, Pat, rap, sad, tap

High-Frequency Words
New
funny, sing, sings

Previously Taught
a, the, what

Pals

page 75

Decodable Words
Target Skill: Short *e*
Ben, den, get, led, Len, let, Mel, pet, Ted, Wes, yes

Target Skills: Consonants *y, w*
Wags, Wes, yes

Words with Previously Taught Skills
big, can, did, dog, has, his, hop, in, is, laps, Lin, log, logs, Mom, on, pal, pals, ran, sat, six

High-Frequency Words
New
all, who

Previously Taught
a, and, be, play, the, with

Ned

page 81

Decodable Words
Target Skill: Short *e*
bed, get, Ned, ten, yes

Target Skills: Consonants *y, w*
wigs, win, yes

Words with Previously Taught Skills
at, bat, big, can, cap, has, hats, his, hit, Hog, hot, in, is, it, nap, not, Ox, Pig, top

High-Frequency Words
New
does, here, who

Previously Taught
a, have, he, no, too

Ken and Vic

page 87

Decodable Words
Target Skill: Short *e*
get, gets, Ken, wet, yes

Target Skills: Consonants *k, v, j*
job, Ken, Vic

Target Skills: Consonants *y, w*
wet, yes

Words with Previously Taught Skills
bag, bat, big, can, dots, has, his, hit, is,
it, sip, tags, tan, top

High-Frequency Words
New
does, here

Previously Taught
a, too, what, with

My Pets

page 93

Decodable Words
Target Skill: Short *e*
bed, den, fed, get, jets, men, pet, red,
set, ten

Target Skills: Consonants *k, v, j*
jets, Kit, Vic

Words with Previously Taught Skills
Big, can, cat, dog, fit, fits, in, is, it, nap,
not, sit, six, tin

High-Frequency Words
New
does, here, me, my

Previously Taught
and, go, the, with

Fun in the Sun

page 99

Decodable Words
Target Skill: Short *u*
fun, sun, tug, up

Words with Previously Taught Skills
can, Ed, has, his, Hog, hop, hops, hot, in, is, Jen, on, Pig, yes

High-Frequency Words
New
friend, hold, pulls

Previously Taught
no, the, too

Yams! Yum!

page 105

Decodable Words
Target Skill: Short *u*
but, up, yum

Words with Previously Taught Skills
bag, bed, big, can, fat, fit, get, has, his, in, is, lots, red, set, ten, Yak, yams, yes

High-Frequency Words
New
full, hold

Previously Taught
a, and, do, he, to, what

Fun, Fun, Fun!

page 111

Decodable Words
Target Skill: Short *u*
Bud, fun, Gus, run

Target Skills: Consonants *qu, z*
Liz, quit, zag, zig

Words with Previously Taught Skills
can, Dad, Deb, is, it, Jen, Jim, Kim,
Mom, not, on, tag, Ted

High-Frequency Words
New
hold

Previously Taught
and, do, have, play, to, with

Bud

page 117

Decodable Words
Target Skill: Short *u*
Bud, cup, dub, fun, hugs, mud, pug,
pup, rub, run, sun, tub, tug, us

Target Skills: Consonants *qu, z*
quit, zip

Words with Previously Taught Skills
big, can, digs, dog, fit, gets, has, hops,
hot, in, is, it, naps, sits

High-Frequency Words
New
good, many

Previously Taught
a, help, play, the, we, with